BOOK NINE
LENA AND PETER IN GERMANY

Garry Popper

ℜℜ
Ravette Publishing

First published in the UK by Ravette Publishing Ltd 2001

Ravette Publishing Ltd
Unit 3, Tristar Centre, Star Road,
Partridge Green, West Sussex RH13 8RA

BIG, BIG WORLD, BIG DREAMS, BIG KIDS
™ & © AMR Popper Associates 2001

Design & Production: Garry Popper. 3d Illustration: Andi Johnson.
Logo Design: Rosalyn Popper.
Picture composition & Layout: Phil Highton. Scanning: Nick Gray

Origination by Qualitype Ltd, Leicester, UK
Printed by Creative Print and Design Group Limited, Heathrow, Middlesex

ISBN: 1-84161-060-7

Lena and Peter live in Germany,
in Frankfurt and Munich -
and Kiel, near the sea!

In so many towns!
Just how can that be?
It's easy when you live
in a circus family!

They're part of a
travelling Acrobatic Troupe
of performing artistes who do
loop-the-loop.

At each village and town
where their caravans stop,
the band strikes a chord
and up goes the Big Top.

In their tent,
Lena and Peter dress up in costumes
while mama and papa prepare their
fine plumes.

To a fanfare in the arena,
their procession parades
and the audience cheers with
loud accolades.

Rising up in the air
to tread the high wires,
they dive and they swoop
through blazing tyres.

Meanwhile,
the crowd holds its breath with delight,
as Lena and Peter do somersaults
in mid-flight.

These daring young fliers
and their incredible feats,
know how to make audiences
cling to their seats.

As the grand finale
draws this show to a close,
will your town be next
where their circus goes?

... Who knows?

Did you enjoy reading about the children in Big World?
If you did, write and tell us about you and what kind of stories you like,
and we will send you a <u>free</u> Big World colouring poster.
Some of the best letters will also be chosen in a special draw.
They will be printed on the back pages in the next series and
seen by children all over the world.

All you have to do is send your letter to:-
"Big World Kids Club"
Ravette Publishing Ltd
Unit 3, Tristar Centre, Star Road,
Partridge Green, West Sussex, England RH13 8RA